STONEDANCE

GW01464811

Writing of his own poetry in 1965 (in *Recent Poetry in New Zealand*) Mike Doyle spoke of the need to move away from 'self-absorbed subjectivism' and romantic diction. He also spoke of the danger of verse-making becoming a habit. This collection, drawn from his work since then, shows an extension, amounting to a breakthrough, of the range and spirited handling of theme, idiom, and language. His poetry moves from the spare, tender lyric, to the multiple levels of reference and metaphor in the long poem, 'Noah'.

Mike Doyle, born in 1928, grew up in England and moved to New Zealand in 1951. In the early 1960s he taught at the University of Auckland. Since 1967 he has been at the University of Victoria, British Columbia. His poetry has been published widely in journals and anthologies in New Zealand, Australia, North America, and Britain; he has published several collections (in earlier years under the name of Charles Doyle); he edited the anthology, *Recent Poetry in New Zealand,* has published a study of R.A.K. Mason in the Twayne World Authors series, and has books forthcoming on James K. Baxter and William Carlos Williams.

# STONEDANCER
*Mike Doyle*

'Music is swallowed by stones' *Joseph Brodsky*

AUCKLAND UNIVERSITY PRESS
OXFORD UNIVERSITY PRESS

*This book is published with
the assistance of a grant from
the New Zealand Literary Fund*

*First published 1976*
*© Mike Doyle 1976*
*Printed in New Zealand*
*at the University of Auckland Bindery*
*ISBN 0 19 647945 2*

*. . . for Meki, too*

## ACKNOWLEDGEMENTS

Landfall
Poetry Australia
New Orleans Review
Yale Literary Magazine
Canadian Forum
Malahat Review
Quarry
Poetry New Zealand
Tuatara
Prism International
Intrepid
Ariel
Ocarina (India)
Second Aeon (Britain)
Beloit Poetry Journal
Alcheringa: A Journal of Ethnopoetics

Exeter Books (England) for poems from my book *Earthshot*
Weedflower Press (Canada) for poems from my book
    *Preparing for the Ark*

Waiata Records, Auckland, New Zealand
Le Bel Enterprises, Edmonton, Alberta, Canada
New Zealand Broadcasting Corporation
Canadian Broadcasting Corporation

# CONTENTS

## MASSAGE WITH GLADIATOR OIL

For the whole man, well-rounded,
seek in Upper Queen Street.
Aided by thick-howled photographs
of fly-specked fellows, oiled
hair, white thighs, white torsos,
a card in a dust-clad window
conjures up miracles of
dumb-bells, trusses, biceps.

Hard by the Town Hall and,
crouched across the street,
the muscularities
of the Methodist Mission,
the unguent is advertised.

Mind's food, also, is handy.
A few windows along (the flies
have got there, too) are displayed
paperbacks: *Love Me Forever,*
*She Laid It On the Line*
and a sequel to *The Naked Lunch*
entitled *We Dress for Dinner.*

For the Aquarian, opposite,
an array of electric guitars,
melodeons, ukuleles,
boxes of green felt picks,
curlicue saxophones.
Nearby the design begins
to shape, in the kindergarten
in a park where the sun
never ceases to shine.

One always hopes for
the classic transformation
to happen before one's eyes:
the skinny weed gingerly
tapping to be let in,
standing back for the hero

*9*

to emerge trussed up in his muscles,
a dumb-bell bulging his biceps,
— but it never happens. Waiting
in one's flabby flesh
one wonders if all this
built-up ends in dumbshows
on window-blinds; cries
from one's heart to the unappearing
heroes, Rub down! Rub down!
Outside the lions roar.

# COSMIC COMMUNICATION

*(with my sons)*

Not rippling, roaring, clay
lumpish is how I see,
or rather sense, myself.

Yet spark or drift moves
towards them. How do they
receive this lumbering

palpable, squabbish flesh?
Young enough, one floats
a smile to me, sharing

water, our first element.
Admittedly, there are spars
sometimes, in choppy breakers,

and, though comfortably far,
rocks; but that smile's repaid
in swans' flight, algae baubles,

water lilies. Once
in the Domain hothouse
one, huge as Ixion's wheel,

spun, striking spume, took fire.
The eldest, there, saw perhaps
that day my hands raised, fork

into flame, me consumed
in my own sulphurous wrath.
Wise, calm, on his via

media does the third
perceive how they conspire
earth, air, fire, water

fashioning child and man?
Rooted, flying, combustible,

floating, drowning,

however he may, he must
(water to clay, fire to clay)
shape them in the one kiln,
make of them what he can.

# AT KAREKARE BEACH

gazing seaward
gripped
by the beach's resonant
silence:
then
to the bush-drowned hills
where, in another history,
body upon body
a whole Maori tribe
was flung two hundred feet
to the rocks below,
thinking of poets
far away, scattered
across America, conscious
of Bill Williams, still
a presence in the touch of love
passed to the loneliest
towns of that continent,
I turned inland again
feeling the sun crouch
close on the hill, burned black now,
the weight of that land's long miles,
knowing that no one
was there. No one was there.

# SHEN KUA'S SPECIFICATIONS FOR TRAVEL

for making comfortable
an official inspection-carriage

arranging its lacquered interior
to get a good view of the scenery, etc.,

In one's travelling cases: a raincoat,
a chest of medicines,

plenty of spare clothes & combs,
a box of preserved foods, & tea

another containing paper, ink, scissors,
a rhyming dictionary & a lute

Candles, knives, chessmen & a folding chessboard
are not to be forgotten

A box should be prepared to receive
books which may be bought en route

together with some insecticide powder
for keeping worms away

Lastly,
'mud-boots' should be taken

as there are some places
which cannot be reached without them

## FLIGHT INTERIOR

Moving back through the aeroplane
shoe toeing for firm floor he glimpses
green fields below him. Walking
on air traverses miles

of land at one step. His foot
hovers above the sea. Travelling
without his seven-league boots
having no gift for walking

on water he is afraid. Vibrations
suffuse him, but his foot comes down
proving the sea flat calm, solid.
Seated he feels the black maw's

foetor engulf him. Is
Jonah. Touching down, he swims
through surf grass to the terminal
drowning in this new element.

## RESPONSIBLE WORLDS

*(after St Exupéry)*

Life responds to life
perfectly

flowers mingle with flowers
in the wind's eye

the swan is the familiar
of all swans

What a space
between men's spirits

Walking with slow steps
eyes lowered

a girl passes homeward
smiling to herself

filled with adorable inventions & with fables
her reverie isolates her from me

how shall I enter into it?

## ONES ONCE ONE

We.  Here.  It snows.
Snow.  Locked in by
ice.  We glad.  Warm.  Good.
We need not go

out.  To the world.  For
those days while the
Snow stays.  To be
here.  Swans.  Two.  A

shared space, small,
white, of peace.  To
stop is not to wait
but to be.  To be

two, but one.  Not
caught, but held:  here.
Snow is now.  Love.
What each flake comes to.

## DREAMING OF GARDENS

'You are some other's fortunate wish'
                          — Irving Layton

Who am I that I should dream of gardens
wanting you in them, your slender berry-brown
body naked among the ardent foliage?

> *I am the one you dream of*
> *when you dream of gardens*

I should tune my fingers over your thighs, dreaming
my caresses' texture, your skin, the border of hair
You lie there waiting and the grass is tender

> *I am the one you dream of*
> *when you dream of gardens*

Moonlight glitters in your narrowed eyes
What is this fruit you offer me? Deliciously
my lips taste upon it your hand's touch. But who

> planted the flowers and tall trees
> in this garden of which you dream?

## MARIGOLDS, CRYSTALS

The marigolds outside
midway through their six-month
season, sun pours glittering
motes, its golden light
rivalling the bedspread's
designing flowers.

On the wooden chair
your things — blouse, slacks,
discarded stockings.
Turning, I see myself
in the oval mirror,
naked. I love
both of us; this stolen
midday; the timelessness
of pure happiness.

When, at last, we
are not together
lamplight is purple
on the distant peak.
And on the hill slope, look
at the beautiful skiers.

See them go, see them go
over the frozen snow.

## NIJINSKY SAID

> *They want me to dance*
> *a merry dance. I do not*
> *like merriment, I like life.*

Sam Goldwyn, mogul,
to Billy Wilder, director:

> *What for we wanna make movies*
> *about some crazy guy*
> *thought he was a horse?*

Wilder, exasperated:

> *Waal, we could have a great*
> *climax scene. Show him*
> *winning the Kentucky Derby!*

Nijinsky wrote in his *Diary:*

> *I am the one who dies*
> *when he is not loved.*

## SIX FEET HIGH AND RISING

sitting at home
   winter evening kitchen
      kids put to bed/think of
glugging at a can of beer
   half listen to Bob
      Dylan, 'Tom Thumb's Blues',
wonder/for the 1000th time
   why am I here? Look back
      glumly/over the 41 years of my life


A rank smell of queen and country is in the air.
Stiff upper lips tremble/in rage and fear at the crass Americans.
      I ponder a sentence from *Cain's Book:*
      *The past is always a lie; clung to by an odour of ancestors.*
I am sick with the way every idea is stifled
in yesterday's dark suit, collar & tie.


      I am puffing quietly.
      Every word comes through to me now —
      slow, precise, the spell.

I watch the grain in the wood of the kitchen cupboards
for the familiar owls' tuwhooing winglessness,
monkeys, popinjays, dys-pep-tic cy-clop-e-an gi-ants
      and as I watch/the grain in the wood
      begins to flow like a 1000 rivers
to build like contours which become mountains
   Kanchenjunga   Fujiyama   Chimborazo
     & I merge into the stream again
     & know in my soul that its waters
   are the waters of content
& I stand on the last tip of the highest mountain
   aware in the beat of my blood
     of all the land spread out below me
     the sunburst kingdom of joy

# HELLO!   IS THAT YOU?   THIS IS ME

day after day      night
after night

having this conversation
with God     long distance

asking him:
God, did Attila the Hun

Voltaire     Nietszche     Abelard
(and other guys on my list

finally make
immigrant status?

Asking him about bad popes
women popes     Errol Flynn

and if there's a football team
up there     and a first eleven

Asking him:
when there's another war in Heaven

what's your policy, G.,
on draft-card burners?

What would you say
if earthmen captured

one of your chariots for trespassing
inside our 12-mile limit?

Questions of moment
asking him

His answers are muffled
voice like chewed frog

but sometimes his favourite question
comes through loud and clear

WHY DID YOU DO IT?   WHY
DID YOU DO IT?

What bothers me —
who'll pay for the call

when I finally hang up?
Or will he cut me off

his dead receiver
leaving me no one to talk to

another bill stacked up to meet
on the due date? Heh! Heh!

When the bailiff comes
I won't be home

only, dangling by its cord
my cherryred telephone

wailing and sputtering    born
without gods    without an answer

## SHAVING

after
another poem's
arrival

               (you beautifully
               reclining
               in the bath)

clearing
steamed-up mirror
with towel I say:

               *I dig those small*
               *thin poems: epiphanies*

               *and long-lined ecstasy*
               *Dionysiac ravings*

               *Can't stand*
               *organized measures*

               *of rational cohesion*
                    *They bore me*

               *Wow! That's a poem!*
               I say

You say:        *At this rate*
               *you're going to grow*
               *a beard*

## GROWING A BEARD

it's a full time
occupation, he said

there's my work cut out
for the summer

since he's a man of discrimination
I imagine it so

him growing it
carefully, hair by hair

## MR D RETURNS, TO THE SCENE
## OF HIS FORMER TRIUMPHS

Believe me, it's been a long time.
Memory can fail.
Nothing remains the same, they say.

As I strolled down Queen Street
after all these years
I saw with proper astonishment
the Town Hall had sprouted a golden cupola,
strobe lights played on the glass dome covering the street,
the sidewalks were ankle deep in pearls,
every girl I saw beautiful as Nefertiti,
lute music scented the air
strummed by angels on the payroll of a big department store
and the burghers all wore diamond-lensed bi-focals.

I couldn't believe it.
Progress, I thought, that's what it is.
These achievements had been held in the hearts of my townsmen
even on the very day I'd bought
a third-class ticket out of town
just to get away from the place,
stopping only on the other side of the planet.

Now, walking back towards the railway station
buoyant with filial pride
I notice the floor of the capacious vestibule
is paved with Carrera marble.
Checking my ticket I find. . .
I've gotten on the wrong train
on the wrong day, & gotten off
at the wrong station, on a railway line
I've never heard of before.
Bastards!   The service is just as bad as ever.

## MIRRORS

### 1

### Reading the Mercury

dusk forms a
picture

gradually
in the window

pane     I sit
hoping it's you come back

It becomes clear
— is only me

peering at
darkness

hoping
it's you
come back


### 2

### Housing Project

Thirsty on a
clear summer night
to the lake
to drink

for a moment
hold the moon
in cupped hands
then in one

gulp

swallow it

## 3

how many evenings
have I visited
empty houses

seen you walking
lovely as ever
on deserted streets

called you to say
I love you

having checked
your number's not in the
'phone book
reassured
you don't
exist

## 4

**Boy on a Trampoline**

higher
he soars and
HIGHER

on the cliff edge
20 or 30 feet
above

waves
nibbling at this shore
10,000 years

waiting

for one brown-eyed boy
to plunge

5

**By the Lake**

on what exponents
of 'fine writing' would call
'a limpid day'

the lake water unimaginably
clear

pitched headlong
the trees
drown in it

and deeper yet
the mountain we
have always wanted to climb

lacking that clarity
longing for that depth
I poise on the shore
nerving myself
to jump in
and soar

to the submerged
sky

6

**Looking out of the window**

and

suddenly
there's nothing

*29*

there

the trees (together
with the seasons they indicated)
have vanished

even the sky — nothing

now the window itself has
gone

chairs tables paintings books

it feels as if the walls
second by second
grow thinner
look at the calendar!
where there were numbers —
blank spaces

today's date
is being snapped off
NOW

in one bite
by an invisible. . .

all that's left — me
standing in the middle
of the last room

not knowing whether
to be glad
or

## NOAH

1. *La fievre fit plus d'animaux que les
ovaires n'en fir jamais*

Henri Michaux

1.                       To choose the right animals,
                         the appropriate species
                         the inevitable individuals
         to avoid awakening on that first morning
         in the gale's dementia to discover your
         creatures suppurating there, or their
         breaths blue with leprous evil

2. Jung and Teilhard both make stones breathe.
   Aphrodite released from a shell. Stones,
   shells. Might some of these not have been chosen?

3. 'Are there giants in this country, daddy?'
   'Are there robbers?'
   'Are there wolves?'
   All timespace NOW for the child. In that one
   instant giant/wolf/robber
                         happens
                                 totally
   Fleeing
         the child
                   relinquishes himself
   Becoming a new self
                       he can never
             find the old one again
   Never forget it.

*31*

4. Earth
once a
shoreless ocean
warm
propagated
'granules of protoplasm'
Teilhard
earth too
emerging
from a womb
Was Noah's a
second birth?
Did he die to the
first life?


5. Ark fashioned from a
square tree
100-120 years in the
making

(then
what happened
to the 'other workmen'
Noah employed?


6. All that water?


7. The raven                    (some say dove
deserting Noah
to gorge on the
bloated floating carrion
(courage
(greed
the vast oceans his metaphor
for hunger

*32*

8. **A Landscape**
   Last birds leaving. The
   trees to be in full leaf
   a few weeks on. Those
   unfelled. Soon
   the saw will scream through
   the last tree. Then
   the last birds will leave
   forever. This wood
   a windswept space of
   stone and scree and
   the bones.


9. Mildew darkens the
   bulkhead


10. Flood, our darkness.
    Without it, no more than
    light.


11. Through his great height
    giant Og of Bashan escaped
    the flood

    Hurtali
    sitting astride
    the ark roof

    awaiting Noah's
    fist full of food
                   (K rations
    thrust through the cubit-
    high window

    Meantime Hurtaliog
    learns from Poumapi and Barabo

limb from limb
how to tear apart his vaporous dreams


12.   Begun and ended in spring
      Ark made of pine
      in proportions of the human body
      90-odd animals, birds, reptiles
                        the whole place stinking of
                                tiger's piss
                        and the farts of baboons
                  Yr continence keeps them by.
                  The burden of being their confessor!



13.   Item: food distribution. Daylight animals to be fed
      at regular times by day. Nocturnal animals by night,
      Og receiving his rations through an aperture in the
      roof. A wearisome chore. Tired to the marrow hearing
      the graunching noise of a beak sharpened against
      cage bars in impenetrable darkness. The candle
      illuminates only raw hands and great sagging lumps of
      red meat. Later only a meat-like gruel from tins.
      Item: living quarters. Beasts and cattle battened
      in the hold, picking their way among cairns of
      dehydrated turd. Middle deck occupied by the birds,
      bloodflecked feathers, points of light burning madness
      upon coagulated night. Promenade deck houses Noah
      and family. Men and women kept strictly apart, Noah
      and sons at the east end, women at the west. Watching
      the walls grow thicker and thicker in damp silence.



14.   The parts clamped
      or gouged out
                  watching
            the structure
                  shaping

its creation a
dismissal
of all past
             Then, too
             man shapes with
                    his own hands.
             much that survives
                    him
       When it is done
       his eyes gaze upon
       a paradox
his own life
his own death
             one
                    the same


15.  Even the windowpanes
                    wept


16.  *All things fall and are built again*
     *And those that build them again are gay*
                    (WBY)


17.  At first it felt
     like immortality
             Then the sound of the rain
             diminished
                    The roar
             died away
     to a steady rhythm
     like a clock
             ticking


18.  Perhaps paradise

is always
what is
        lost?


19.  The gods
     Struldbrugs
     Cryonics
                to waken to
                a day not
                our own
     God speaking to Noah. Tells him to make an Ark of gopher
     wood (or pine or). Noah thought: I shall survive
     almost everything which now exists. Caulking with
     pitch. Sealing his own fate. Apprehension of the
     unknown 'sea'. Might it not already hold strange
     mysterious spirits ready to dominate the afterworld?
     One window cubit-high. Weeping. Cyclopean. The
     raven's egress. Sane link. Without it, this Ark
     the truly psychotic being.


20.  Three tiers (tears)
        storeys
                body
                mind
                spirit


21.  One door for the entry of wife, sons (death, antithesis,
     enmity, life's only ultimate meaning, profound love),
     sons' wives, the pairs
                        of animals
     One window
                to witness the rising
     waters
                pleas, curses
                of the drowning

*36*

22. Noah could be finally saved only if his Faustian
    heart were torn from his side


23. Preparations for the ark. The parents of Jacques
    Emile Blanche were wealthy, in part from running
    a private lunatic asylum.
        Madame Blanche said: 'We have a hundred
    thousand francs a year, not counting our dear lunatics'.


24. Human, are not the responsibilities placed on Noah
    too great? For the carpenters at Gerona, Salerno,
    the four in the silver altar panel in Pistoria
    Cathedral, and the sailmaker of Regensburg. For the
    syphilitic vulva of the future.


25. Had Noah been an artist, his destiny would have been to
    drown with the others.


26. Noah's salvation and renewal not in themselves final.
    He retained and was returned to his human nature.
    Adam remembered Eden, longed for it. Noah's memory
    is of the prelapsarian world God had condemned.


27. Ark: snail. Univalve shell. Origin in ocean.
    Habitats: woodland, pasture, pool, large bodies/
    of water, under rocks, in mosses, on cliffs,
    underground, in trees, in warmish springs.
        Some fossil gastropods 5-6 ft long (now ½-3″).
        Sluggish, sedentary, hard shells, slow locomotors.
        Protection: shell, coloration, secret habits.
    Eaten by birds, beetles, small mammals, fish and other

predators. Often harmed by larval stage parasites
who house in them.
        Snails live on plants. Have two retractile tentacles
        with eyes on, and a mouth.
        Hermaphroditic.
Usually most active at night, when they glide by
wavelike contractions of the foot muscle. Slime gland
located at anterior end of foot deposits mucous film
over which snail moves 10-12 ft per hour.
        In very dry weather they form temporary covering
        (epiphragm) of mucus over shell aperture.
        Live under leaves or in burrows.
        Radula used for rasping off food.
Like the damp.


28.    Rubber man, bulbous, globular, skin brother to whale,
       walrus, octopus. Heaven of hulls (planets floating
       in the aqueous firmament). Phosphorescent fish.
       Cold algae. Slow motion. Grass in the (water) wind.
       Our life too swift for him. Our laughter tears his
       dry throat.


29.    'Lithocardites are heart shells, rough draughts of
       a heart that one day will beat' (Bachelard); and
       Swift to Pope: 'I value not what becomes of posterity
       when I consider from what Monsters they are to spring'
                (2.xii.1736)


30.    And Madame de Maintenon
       by the pond at Marly:
               'See how languid the carp are;
               like me they regret
               their mud'.

31.  Body as sea
     *mare nostrum*

                    soul as ark
                    afloat upon it


32.  'I didn't die . . . Everything that I had was taken away
     from me and I didn't die. I could do nothing.
     Nothing. Strange that I could do nothing. No.
     There was nothing I could do'. *(The Pawnbroker)*


33.          fossils in shale
             how the mind
             baulks and flinches

             numinous pictures in
             the knifeblades so
             sky without end

             when it meets
             sea in the seen distance
             two azures

             blend at infinity
             mind forks, blenches
             in the thunderous cloud


34.                     carried
                    out to sea
                         swallowed
                 in the dark belly
                    journeys from west to east
                       path of the sun's
                 transit from sunset to dawn
                          a death
                                 Light

35. Ark: precautions. Dream of being in a house with a
small group of other (unidentified) people, defending the house
(or, alternatively, using it as a vantage point of attack).
The opposition, whom we fire upon with rifles (hunting guns)
is partly in the street, partly in a house opposite. Dream
ends with the realization that both back door and front door
of our house are *ajar*          (May, 1968).


36. Ark: the animals. Outside, slaver and howl the excluded hyenas.
Within, high-pitched squeak of the bat navigating the dark-flood
world. Hindus place elephant and lion higher than man. Yet it
is sd: 'The Unicorn often fights with elephants.' And the
lion may fear the white cock and the scorpion.
     Sorrow-eyed caged melancholy lynx at Duncan; his piss w
never become a jewel.
     Sort of penis dream: arms bitten off by shark, lion.
     *Nothing more solemn on earth than a dance of trained dog*
                              (Conrad)
     Children of Lir, transformed by jealous Eva into four
                    white swans
          Argos a golden peacock
                         wounded with precious stones
Antinous feeding
          the wing-clipped wrens to the great python
               in its filigree basket
                    in the temple of Zeus
                    at Athens
Falcons plummeting at Samosata
driving herds of antelope into purple nets
                         A bee droning from
                         flower to flower
                         searching for the primal house
                         where his birth and death
                         sweetness, energy
                         are one and one and one
          Who shall be whole again
          without the sweet breath of the panther?

*40*

37. Moored barges. Casks. Portuguese tuns. Black coals, sleeping. Wind running in the harsh linen of the sailors. Jasper green as the sea-depths.

38.
       To Xisuthus
       10th King of Babylon
       the god Cronus
       appeared in a dream
       warned him that all men
       would be destroyed in a flood
       on the 15th day of the
       month Daesius, which is
       the Macedonian calendar . . .

39. It was ingeniously conjectured by Sir Henry Rawlinson that the 12 cantos of the Gilgamesh epic corresponded to the 12 signs of the zodiac, so that the course of the poem followed, as it were, the course of the sun through the 12 months of the year. The theory is to some extent confirmed by the place assigned to the flood legend in the 11th canto; for the 11th Babylonian month fell at the height of the rainy season, it was dedicated to the storm-god Ramman, and its name is said to signify 'month of the curse of rain'.

40. When the waters abated Deucalion and Pyrrha repopulated the world by throwing stones over their shoulders. Deucalion's stones became man, Pyrrha's women. Or was it the mud at Iconium?

41. . . . nest, chrysalis and garment constitute one moment of a dwelling-place. The more concentrated the repose, the more hermetic the chrysalis, the more the being

*41*

that emerges from it is a being from elsewhere . . .


42.  Tired, Noah battened the
     ultimate hatch, wood
     already somewhat swollen from
     wet. Much thought, heavy labour
     had gone to choosing and sorting
     his companions, the animals.
     Now he lay down, rainsound
     soothing him to sleep.
          He awoke refreshed
     to discover, close to his face
     a terrifying monster he had not chosen.
     At the foot of his bed
     someone
     had placed a mirror.


43.  Drunken and naked, Noah,
          looking into the eyes of the future


44.  An ant, iridescent green, its metallic quality reflecting
     the early summer sun, exploring crevices of a cedar log
     on the beach. Log's outer surface weathered, silvered.
     Within, it is a pale dry-looking brown and, where it is
     gouged to that depth, filled with black or darkgreen
     seasmooth pebbles.
          The water is a pale shimmering pearlgrey haze, flatcalm
     except for a light offshore breeze making herringbone
     patterns on the surface. Across the water, snow whitens
     the mountain peaks. A single heron stands in the shallow
     tidewater. To the right the skyline is ragged with pine
     trees. Flood long subsided. Seagulls fly low above the
     shoreline, squawking rhythmically, intent for scraps.
     Everywhere rocks and stones deepgreen with moss. The
     further outlook is dry.

45. The ends of the rainbow rooted in the soil of the new world grow again and again as flowers.

46. Alfred Jarry, on his deathbed and barely conscious, asked if there was anything he wanted, gave a slow, thoughtful smile and said, 'Yes, a toothpick'.

## GOING ON WITH THE POEM

*The white dove flew*
*from the dark field of night*
like breathing. Even in that
something to learn. How to go
deeper. Or swimming. An instinct
billion years in the blood, but
brought (*from the dark*)
again to the surface. Or
diving. Go in too deep
you may have visions, never
recover, or
the bends, 'despondency
. . .madness'.

       Good
to imagine it, poem as breathing.
The simple act of being, yet
made of words through which no
clarity is lost. Once or
twice the simple miracle
may occur. Otherwise
it is like unfolding
the layered petals of a flower.
Or the small thing, remaking
another poet — tenth
pressing of the grape —
as now when a line
so given will not leave me,
plunging deeper far than
its occasion:

*The white dove flew from the dark field of night*

What is being given me?
Who is the giver?
Is there more I am missing?
Perhaps the *more* shines
too brilliant for me to see?

*The white dove flew from the dark field of night*

like an echo through the poem
of my life
intimations
*from the dark field of night*
of *kairos*
*the white dove*
The One Poem.

# THE COMB AND THE SWORD

*(for Vincent O'Sullivan)*

Tall girl, bronze mirror, hair
swept in her comb, sea-wave
in sunlight's moving beam:
that pride in itself beautiful,
excitement at the beauty she looks upon.

You set the scene at Troy. Well
enough. Coiled at her throat
the snake-brooch, a foreboding?
Lurking nearby the figure
of Cruelty, blade in hand.

The moral:   cruellest,
young beauty wantonly destroyed
at its moment of full flowering?

In a bladeless world that girl
hair by hair would lose
loveliness. In the slow stroke
of comb through hair, in the tides
of water & light, rising,
falling, rising & falling,
in her hand shifting the comb
stroke upon stroke. That's where cruelty is.

## THE TREE

*(after Magritte)*

growing from the earth towards the sun,
is an image of a certain happiness.

To see this you must be absolutely still
like the tree. When we are moving
it is the tree which watches us.

Equally, in the shape of chairs,
tables, and doors, it witnesses
the agitated spectacle of our life.

Having become our coffin
it disappears into the earth.

And when it is transformed into fire
the tree vanishes into the air.

## WATCHTOWER

Hovering in my kitchen doorway
holding a black book in one hand
& two pulp magazines in the other
he gravels from his hoarse throat:

> *Apocalypse in four years!*
> *Next act's Armageddon.*
> *Only the few will be saved.*

I believe him, too. The world's
in such lousy shape, with Richard
Burton & Liz Taylor for king & queen
& the Americans torturing &/massacring
another bunch of orientals.
What a world! Hugh Hefner
promoting liberty & Nixon
making everything perfectly clear.

The only distraction from its perfect
horror & ugliness, I glimpse
through the kitchen window/ a flock of quail
moving beautifully & together
across the grass. Almost, seen at distance,
rolling, smoothly. I be heartened
to see them, & one pause, shake
wings, move on. The voice of doom
continues. . .

But Doran comes in, looks from the window, says

> *There are some quail running across.*
> *They're much more spaced out than they normally are.*

The print in the magazines turns brown as quail feathers
They fly from the man's hand.
He runs after them, chasing
The Book of Revelation over the springy grass.

We watch the sky for its pages to turn white

& the snow forecast for this morning
to sweep toward our quiet, a
flock of released doves.

## THE SPADE

*(for Doran)*

A spade stands upright
in the weed-choked soil. I choose
to peer at twinings of wistaria,
speckles of stones, and tidy
into a burning-pile fir branches
ripped and scattered by equinoctial
winds. Later in the season
there'll be things to do. The watering.
Grass to shave. Blackberry
to chop back. Perhaps then I'll shift
that spade from the perpendicular
my body quickening to its thrust and lift.

Today, the first day of your absence,
I sit and contemplate the possibility.

# FOUR NOTES FROM A DREAMBOOK

## 1. Doran's Dream

'I think it's fear
of aging. My teeth falling
out. My mouth full
of loose teeth & lost ear-rings'.


## 2. Dream in the Hotel Georgia, Vancouver

                Doran & me
                        high
            in Kansas City
            on the hundredth floor
            of the Macrocosmic Hotel

            the blank cream walls
                    suddenly
                            concave

            an instant
            of brilliant
                        sky


## 3. Dog

            the forest fingers me
            suddenly its green sinews
            burst asunder

            towering beside me
            gigantic malevolent red dog
            fire-fanged

            This is the dog
            to be given into my charge

            He moves toward me

I reach out toward him

He grows larger, larger

My hand touches. I have him, I have him—

a large, soft, gold-coloured dog,
shaggy-haired, mild-eyed.


## 4. On Cordova Bay Ridge

Night of no cloud
full moon

drove downslope
on this closed street

encompassed the moonshaped
turning circle

eyed the great moon in the sea
shimmering

dreamed
of a flaming structure like a gallows

two legs of flame
topped by a hoop of white
flames
        set
on the black road
just above the turn
& the great white trembling moon
                                above

In threes
circle of moon
turning circle
hoop of white flame
                    flickering

*52*

The task
message of the gods
to leap through that small tight inward licking
hoop of flame

but I stood there helpless
immobile
a stone which would strike no spark
as the hoop grew smaller & smaller

I could not move

the last fierce brightness of that quenching flame
burns, burns in my head

## ON A PHOTOGRAPH OF A NUDE PROFILE
## BY KYOJI YANO

that long curved slender back
in shadow
           delicate nail
exquisite talon
           offering
ecstasies
           yet
merely pointing to
           refinements
of chin, pouting     lips
subtle aquilinities     nose
haughty poise     head
hair caught back
           nuances
of colour happily left
           to be imagined

oh Kyoji
           the crook of that slender arm
oh Kyoji
           that your lens should stop
midway
           on the delicate curve of buttock
oh Kyoji
           the dark beautiful belly your camera
keeps from us
           the moderate
breast     uptilted nipple

oh Kyoji
           that long curved slender back
how many of us
           have you bewitched
that we fall in love with a shadow
oh Kyoji

## KLEE AT KAIROUAN

His painted eggs
hidden in the garden
among the sad palms

Oh, the colours of air & sea,
the sultry tide
at noon, & the clear

stars & immense moon,
the blue & gold hearse
& the mourning women

Eggs in the green bushes
& at Kairouan he said
*I am possessed by colour*

*I do not need to pursue it*
*I know that it will possess me forever.*
*I and colour are one.*

## KLEE UND ARP

Arp delighted in
the 'Exciting Animals'

Klee
was very much moved

Klee took his violin
from its case & began to play

Arp told of his father's
Swiss factory

Klee, now listening
stroked a cat curled in his lap

Arp, talking, did not notice
Klee was removing fleas from the fur

Klee, with a flick of his wrist
squashed them against a corner of the table

## ARP & RICHTER MEET
## ON THE ZURICH BAHNHOFSTRASSE

'You see!', Richter exclaimed, 'That's what I look for.
The elements of the tree, its essence.
The living skeleton'.

               In front of the Hotel Elite,
counterpoint to the formal architecture
the cut back, knuckled plane trees
spoke to him in their own language,
their bare, wild outstretched hands gesturing towards him.

Arp replied, caressing the air with his hand
as if stroking a woman's body,
                    'I love the skin'.

## CEZANNE IN OLD AGE

*I believe I become*
*more lucid*
*before nature. . .*

*It is sad not to be able*
*to take many specimens*
*of my sensations & ideas.*

*Look at that cloud — I*
*would like to be able to paint that.*
*Now, Monet, he could do it.*

*He has the muscles. . .*
From hard stone to the
blue fields of the moon

a region of blurred
vision, an aching back,
occasional ecstasies.

## THE WIVES OF THE KING OF KARAGWE

encouraged
by a guard wielding a fat whip

suck through a tube
a constant supply of milk

unable to balance
on their bloated legs

human seals
flapping and wallowing

souls      abandoned
among great breasts and vast buttocks

dreaming of watery poisons
of time grown thin.

Oh, the plump hours!

# ARC

'Next to his pantry, Noah built an aviary
where he kept all the songbirds so that
they could comfort him with their sweet
singing during the perils of the long voyage'


BELOW
            black tar-
    water
            the ball
                            spinning
                            bubbling

    of earth

                'a fragrance of neglect
                still lingers, like a ghost of fallen grass'

when the high clouds        stop
& sun glint no longer catches
                        dew on the  spiders'
                        webs in the first
                                        morning
'the musky opulence of the summer
                            woods,
    where so many birds are dying'

                &

'the frail bones of generations'

    'sifting down now
    into the deep humus of the woods'

        ABOVE
                white disc, wafer
                & offering
                        of moon

'We are the killers. We stink of death. We carry it with us.
It sticks to us like frost'
                    — but forests root vigour &
                              clean crystal of frost


                                        lost


                                             to us
                                             & us



           alas & also


                        space


                        & time


& this the song
                        brewing perhaps forever
                        in the kitchen of
                                        circumstance

accumulations of the soul
                        sores &
                             soars

a     void     a ver-
              ity
                        fragrances of a tended
                                    garden
& we
           BETWEEN

# CABIN ON PORCUPINE RIVER

bucketing the rapids
crawling the mountains
hacking their way
branch by branch, almost
three thousand miles, through the forests

the two prospectors, partners

> frozen rock-solid
> beside a stew kettle dangling
> over a long-dead fire
> (the kettle contains
> a pair of moccasins, partly-cooked,
> embedded in a cake of ice)

have held these attitudes
through the slow ooze & drip
three-quarters of a century

What will they do
in some cryonic future
at the moment of thaw
on the day of judgment?

will all that pent-up hunger
drive them to the steaming stew
or to the gold pan
the rough caress of gravel
the bright cold river's treasure?

moment by moment
imperceptibly
a decision is forming
a decision is forming
in the slow glaciers of their consciousness

## THE HOUSE OF LIFE

First her husband, then her baby daughter
perished.   Inconsolable
for herself, she invoked a medium.
The dark lady declared: 'You will not die
while you are building
a house to live in.   Build
& you will not die.'

                      That very day
she began, building, first in her head.
the imaginings, next
blueprints, clearing of ground,
foundations, the convolutions
& ramifications of her desire
to outbuild eternity.

Brick upon brick, dollar
by dollar she built
fortunes, for the contractors,
for the bankers: five million dollars
for (among other things) a thousand
windows imported from Italy
each one a different size.

Within the shell, first
doors, hundreds of them,
wardrobe doors opening
to blank walls, doors of rooms
giving entrance to the sky.
Then stairs. After a dozen
flights to the ceiling, close
to the buzz of trapped
butterfly wings, she broke
for the open, building
staircases to merge with the towering cumulus,
& then, tiring of vaguenesses in that direction,
she curved her balustrades
down into the ocean, furnishing
her aquamarine apartments with kelp & sea anemone

before turning inward again
bent on creating
rooms within rooms
& rooms within rooms within rooms
acre upon acre.

All the while she was building
sea's impingements shifted the vast foundations,
termites ticked in their dark dry tunnels,
worms oozed in the wet cement
of their own purposes, looping
towards the smallest room
triple-locked, at the dark centre,
where a fine dust of plaster
covered the long box packed
with jumbled bones from a male skeleton,
& poured, faster & faster,
powdering the air, whitening
the treasured coil of her dead daughter's hair.

# WE KNOW WHAT THE ANIMALS DO

(Ojibway Indian beliefs)

what are the needs of the beaver
what are the needs of the bear
what are the needs of the salmon
what are the needs of many creatures

because long ago men married them
because long ago men acquired this knowledge
long ago from their animal wives
men acquired this knowledge

today the priests say we lie, but we know better
the white man has lived in this country only a few short years
the white man knows very little about the country
the white man knows very little about the animals

what are the needs of the beaver?
what are the needs of the bear?
what are the needs of the salmon?
what are the needs of many creatures?

we have lived here thousands of years
we were taught long ago by the animals themselves
the white man writes everything down in a book
so he will not forget it        so he will not forget it

our ancestors married the animals
our ancestors learned all the ways of the animals
our ancestors passed their knowledge on
generation by generation, down to us

what are the needs of the beaver
what are the needs of the bear
what are the needs of the salmon
what are the needs of many creatures

we have lived here thousands of years
we were taught long ago by the animals themselves

our ancestors married the animals
our ancestors passed their knowledge on to us

we do not forget it

# SIBERIAN CURES

(derived from Levi-Strauss, *The Savage Mind*)

for instance: spiders & whiteworms
swallowed as a cure for sterility
among the Helmene & Iakoute;
fat of black beetle (Ossete, hydrophobia);
squashed cockcroach, chicken's gall
(Russians of Sourgout, abscesses and hernias);
macerated redworms (Iakoute, rheumatism);
pike's gall (Bouriate, eye complaints);
loach & crayfish swallowed alive
(Russians of Siberia, epilepsy & all diseases);
contact with a woodpecker's beak,
blood of a woodpecker, nasal
insufflation of the powder,
gobbled egg of the bird *koukcha*
(Iakoute, against toothache, scrofula,
high fevers & tuberculosis respectively);
partridge's blood, horse's sweat
(Oirote, hernias & warts);
pigeon broth (Bouriate, coughs);
powder made of the crushed feet
of the bird *tilegous* (Kazak,
bite of mad dog);
dried bat worn around the neck
(Russians of Altai, fever);
instillation of water
from an icicle hanging on the nest
of the bird *remiz* (Oirote, eye complaints).

. . .among the Bouriate: the flesh of bears
has seven distinct therapeutic uses,
the blood five, the fat nine, the brains twelve,
the bile seventeen, the fur two.
It is also the bear's frozen excretions
which the Kalar collect
at the end of the winter season
to cure constipation.

## MR D DETERMINES ONCE MORE TO ASK HER TO MOVE IN PERMANENTLY

*(with an aside to the shade of Paul Blackburn)*

A year she  has been away
& last time only a short visit
She hardly got warmed up
            blew me a kiss or two
            before leaving

Since then (you were right, Paul)
she's been given the eye by
            1 tallow-haired student
            1 housewife in steel curlers
            1 'artist' with watery, shifty eyes
            & god knows how many secret
            indulgers in business suits

O I dig the way she moves
lightly, the long legs
            carry a neat well-rounded ass,
            lithe waist & grapefruit breasts
Will she give it all to me this time?

Her long blonde hair in the sun
as she eases in on the shining wave
her tanned luminous flesh against
            the white-ribbed shell,
her coming causes quite a stir in me.

Ms Universe, my Beauty Queen, Ms Muse!
I MUST NEVER LET YOU GO AGAIN!

In the back of my head I remember
            those dull mornings when
                        we are both spent
            I watch the curve of her
                        back as she leaves
                                    our shared bed
            But nothing will stir me

                    from near sleep
          As she closes the door gently
                    I turn over to dream
                              of the glorious past
This I remember.  But now
          She has arrived.   She has just arrived
I arrange the wine & roses
          on the festive table.

## DOUBLING BACK

'Just a minute', he'd say,
& go back to make sure
he'd turned off the stove, put out
the lights & the cat, locked
the door, & hidden the key.

Walking westward near sunset
he would turn repeatedly
wanting to know for certain
his shadow was still there.

Not finding any place
which could dispel
his fear of the dark
he would totter on through the night
blindly, afraid of being buttonholed
by a familiar ghost who'd say,
'Just a minute, please'.

At dawn still facing west
peering over his shoulder
he'd break into a run
worrying, wondering why
he was being followed,
shadowed by the sun.

## GOLDEN AGE

Some twinkle in stupors
of roseate foretime.
Not he.  Compelled
to a palsied view, he
chutters, grouching
of weather, the felons
of memory, the great
rains & betrayals
fifty years dried
out. Frayed weskit
dappled with droolings,
his hearing calling forth
querulous bellowings,
his churning responses
the whispers of a giant
fallen, long ago fallen
on evil days, he bad breathes
that stinking mumble-jumble
of mendicants, fellow-
pensioners, sopping
the stale of existence
on pulpy gums . . .so blind now,
blinder than ever,
he can't see himself
for himself.

# AN ASSURED POSITION, A CUTTING EDGE

*(for David Dowling)*

Grass to be cut, as he sits there
grass to be cut. As he sits there
among its gigantic opalescences
ants tug & tumble, scuttering
in nervy orderliness, a fat bee
enters its magic cave of petals,
faint breezes stir a muzzy sun,
but below remain the ambiguous
shadows.   Poised on taut haunches
he peers at a summery world through
thick windows, grime-charted tracts
of dusty territory. Dark-mandibled
a fly explores terrain, a glacier
maybe in its cosmos, or a lake
of warm ice, & drowned in it
deep, a vast pinkfleshed creature under
the treads of its black feet, sideways
to its perceptions, & adjacent
at the same peculiar angle green
forests, teeming, tremorous
with insect regiments. He shifts his hand
under its hard water, a limb rising
from the cryonic depths. Edging
its green horizon the blades, menacing,
advance – slow, to be sure, but guaranteed.
Is he the god, fly-god, prayed to
to blunt in his pink web what threatens?
Or simply a being in his own scale, fixed
in the appropriate position, waiting
(his arms flung out like wings, backward)
the larger, keener-edged knife, the final arc?

# A SEASON OF RITES

With sly demonic grins
urged by their flesh's triumphs
they used to bait him — taut, emotional
catatonic, his tight nates
finding no ease in the nightly
upright armchair, gathering
no clue from his endless staring
at the cheap print of Van Gogh's ear
facing him from the bare wall at eye level

laughing, tickling together,
they seemed to fondle his discomfiture
but could not egg him to enjoy the party.
'He got no balls', she told her latest lover,
& he'd only a shrivelled eye to go without them.
Certainly, he appeared to consummate
nothing but misery.
                    A season of rites
later, emerging, erupted
from her glowing caverns, her latest lover brooded
alone in his still room, his narrow bed
unslept in. He had husbanded
her vast capacities, but could not remain
for long in that dark forest, that deep must,
before discovering everywhere
the scent of a fresh-minted paramour,
his own limp image, wilted,
in the new-banked fires of her one red, kindling eye.

# THE INQUISITOR

*(for Maurice Gee)*

To begin with he knew nothing,
but he had stood
for forty-eight hours erect on two crooked stones,
stung with a sjambok whenever he shifted
or, hungry for sleep, his eyes closed, a brimming
bucket of water just out of reach of his wooden lips.

Still he would doze for a moment
to dream he was being interrogated, teetering,
in a white room where the bone-naked bulb
burned on his skull, on two crooked stones. . .
suddenly, bludgeoned awake by the sjambok's biting
buttock or thigh, he would find the electrodes'
cool metal clipped to his ears, squinching
his testicles, hear a whirring, feel bursting
time & again through his jacknifing body, the surging voltage.
His teeth clattered aloud, cutting his tongue to pieces,
filling his mouth with blood. Then followed intervals
for the interrogation, the convulsions,
and one time, curled like a foetus on the urine-stinking
mattress, feeling the sparks crackle out of his eyeballs.

To begin with he knew nothing
but he soon learnt.
He learnt everything there was to know
concerning his torturers and, in an odd way,
concerning himself, the remarkable identities.

After the first time his difficulty
was that he could never remember
once they switched on the huge floodlight
or attached the coiled hemp to his handcuffs & looped it over
the crossbar near ceiling height, cranking the winch
to jerk him up to the stud, to let him drop
& instantly, stop, with a jolt, so that his toes dangled
clearing the floor by a hopeless inch or two —
he could never remember

74

what it was he had learnt.

Nor did it help him when they plunged his head
into the bucket of water tasting of salt & piss,
or spreadeagled his carcase, bound hand & foot,
across a tractor tyre, his nostrils plugged,
&, covering his mouth with a cloth, poured water into it
through a tube, clogging his throat, almost drowning him.
None of this helped him remember
what it was he had learnt; he did not know
what they wanted to know.
One of his torturers in particular,
clad in neat shorts & kneelength boyscout socks,
spoke softly to him, vowing his disagreement
with how their chaps had 'conducted the enquiry'.
'Only tell us what we want to know', he pleaded,
'and you are free'. But what did they want to know?
Nor could he tell why it was, if it was so,
that this same man, turned beast or demon,
later twisted his spine with an iron bar.

While he was under their care
he felt an intimacy with them, a strange brotherhood.
He could interpret the significance
of each one's slightest gesture
& learned in consequence something about himself,
what sort of creature he would have been
under certain favourable conditions.

One day, or night, time was no longer a question,
he heard the Chief Torturer say:
'It's the rebellious ones I like best. Somehow
it's more of a pleasure to see them broken'.

What he did not know
was what they wanted to know.

He overheard a voice he did not recognize
yet sensed ghosted his own, whispering,
hoarse, slow, as if pondering:
'*Ja baas, ja baas, ja baas, ja baas, ja. . .*',

but he did not know what it assented to.

It was nobody's fault
that, as far as life is concerned, by the end of it
he knew everything else there was to know.

## BLACK DINNY

dwelt in the coalhouse.
Lurked at peripheries
of childhood games, hovering
to topple on scrumping
banger-in-letterbox, hooky-playing
lads. Mongol, tyrant, great
head wobbling, eyes intermittently
seeking portentous sky, legs
spindly below the pot-
belly. Mostly his gat-toothed
stout blackthorn pivoted mother
attended him in dusk streets;
but sometimes alone, lurching,
lumbering, stuttering, uttering
quiet but explosive oaths
(small depth charges) he clambered
past spring or summer's whitewashed
cottages, to Doolan's boozer.

Once we found him
after a spring shower, bundled
drunk in the gutter, soaked,
covered with apple blossom
petals & leaves, like a pig
festooned & garlanded
on the hook after slaughter.

In winter we never saw him
stagger past misted panes
but sometimes pictured a slaked
round-bellied upturned stick-legged
spider dumped among slowly-
dampening nuggets of coal.

# 'A BODY OF THE BLIND. . .'

*Gwen John to John Quinn, 1916 letter*

A man goes before crying
*Faites place!   Faites place!*
& the poor men follow
holding on
holding on to one
        to one another
the luminous clock
unseen, & the moon
above them & through
the skylight, light of the sky,
a black square. They tread
step upon step the heavy
air, singing, sweet & low

       *I dreamt of gold & jewels*
       *& for sure it was no wonder*

but over & over, mechanical
dolls, a tactile
map bulging each pocket,
& everyone's contours
his own landscape
*Faites place!   Faites place!*

The tongue of the air up there
lolls, parched.  Aaah, they pray,
let us be turned to stone
& exist, no – live live, in a
new dimension, even the smoke
can be chipped away
gradually, true, & with effort
but piece by piece the air
may be cleared, the way
be made clear. *Faites place!*
*Faites place!*   Oh, Dan Gullet,
hear me among the rafters!
You up front of the thin

line, above me, hear me.
With the comb of my words part
your hair. When we arrive
*Faites place!   Faites place!*
you who are not in full
darkness do not be dazzled
by the sudden light.  Kneel
for me, for all of us, tell them
up there under the sloping gable
*We'll make it to the finish!*
*Faites place!*   Though our knees
be worn to the bone & bleeding
we are climbing still. We desire
the vision, the dance. *Faites place*!
*Faites place!   Faites place!*

## MR D FIRST SEES HIS PHOTOGRAPH
## THREE YEARS AFTER IT WAS TAKEN

Thank God I've shaved off the beard.
That thicket of whitish-grey bristle!
Can it really be me!
I don't look like that now.
I didn't look like that when I was young.
I looked better when I was young.
I looked younger when I was young!
Remember the beautiful bone structure
of that face? What have these jowls
flanking that ridiculous goatee
to do with me? You say
I'm looking younger all the time
but that's, isn't it, only because I've shaved?
I used to be slim. I used to look forward
to the future. That's why I grew
& grew a beard. Maturity. But now,
after the beard, yes, I am looking, yes,
younger. Growing that beard
was like making a sortie into No-Man's-Land
to discover that some features, some properties,
no one wishes to cultivate.

## DRUNK

Babble it sounded, breathy
babble. No sensible creature
gives ear to muddled maunderings
borne on beery breath. Yet
listen, sssh, listen. . . .his tongue
curls around spells his ragged-arsed
trousers would seem to mock.
Listen. He murmurs in syllables
lifted from legends, filched
from poets. Down-at-heels
drunken babbler he may be, but
prince among magical dialects,
king of the word.

## WOODSIDE ROAD

Seeing the rough box's
white exterior &, cramped to the fence,
tamarisk once planted small
& delicate by your careful
hand, & seeing
besides figtree & passionfruit,
hibiscus, bougainvillea,
& that strange tree
now recognized as the white-flowered
dogwood (emblem
of a later province),
the paint peeling, the grass
choked with weed, I feel
flower again in some part of myself
your beautiful younger body
moving within that shell of white-
painted weatherboards, or my hand
raised to flaunt the first banner
of whiteness on our fresh life,
or, brushed by dewy nipples,
myself poised above rich soil
eager to cast the first seed.

# ONE FOR THE ROAD, OR TWO TO STAY

Was it for this
we travelled, all
these years together,
to tell each other
that what might have been
love, love, has begun
to whither?

What to think of
it, this lesson,
lessening? How
from high romance
to have fallen
through six children
& five counties
to this dark, slow dance?

Let us look, though, once more
in our shared cellar.
Even now remember,
though gorged on the plump
grapes of young affection,
prudent, we may have saved
the fullest wine until
gross appetite's discarded
its first, careless edge.
Here. Let us rest &
from this dusty bottle
drink together. Slanté.

## SEA – KINGS

Pitched steep, tight-wound
through dusty bush
the gravelled road
affords us dunes
& inlet. After
a wooden bridge
we halt, giddy.

Salt tang & creeping
marram usurp
dune upon dune. Iron
glint speckles the packed
margin. Footshapes
track it. At last
breakers, volcanic
rock – sea spray,
petrified spray.

Fishermen sentry
the point. Surfers
ride the high breakers.
Safer, nearer inshore,
we preside, body-
surfing the white foam,
not caring who's king
of the darker fathoms, farther out.

# THE JOURNEY OF MENG CHIAO

*Who says that the heart of an inch-long plant*
*Can requite the radiance of full Spring?*

My carriage has been waiting at the door
for a long time. I am going
on a far journey. I can't be sure
how well the carriage is appointed
for my purposes. It isn't clear to me
what my purposes are. Returned travellers
report that I must pass through a region of darkness.

Why am I leaving the comforts of this fortress?
I cannot give you a reason. Or perhaps this:
I lie awake at nights in the scent of jasmine
recalling the flowers' opening, the day's sunlight,
conversations of my acquaintances,
the discarding of the straw dogs after ritual,
the affairs of the nine orifices and six viscera.

Demon faces emerge when the petals unfold.
Voices trading in small-talk have tongues of fire.
Every transaction seems a sham to me.
Travelling into the depths of my country, inward
further and further, I shall take no companions.
Maybe there will be many strange seas to cross
but this is a journey I need for myself alone.

Beyond what I have said here I can give you no reasons.
The Country of No Love is full of reasons
and they make nothing clear. I have no reasons.
When the Tao is revealed to me there will be no reasons.
I must leave you here by the pinewoods under the sky.
I must go now. What do I hope to find when I arrive?
If I am lucky, the pinewoods under the sky.